TITLE II-A

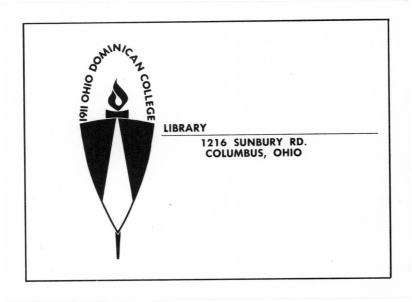

LIBRARY
1216 SUNBURY RD.
COLUMBUS, OHIO

Gorilla Gorilla

Gorilla Gorilla

by Carol Fenner

illustrations by Symeon Shimin

Random House 🏠 New York

The publisher is grateful to Dr. and Mrs. George B. Schaller
for their generous assistance in the preparation
of this book.

For Faith

with whom I still share
a wild and gaudy
special sister laughter

He was born, wet and tiny
and gray,
one wet and gray morning
when the mists lay heavy in the rain forest.
His mother carried him close
in her big arms,
warm in her glossy hair.
His mouth was open a lot.
His appetite was endless.

Before many months
he could ride on his mother's back,
clutching
the hairs on her shoulders
while she moved about with the others,
feeding among the wild celery and thistles
or in the places of bamboo.

He grew.
His hair became long,
covering his body.
He learned which leafy greens
were tasty
and where to find the tender parts of bamboo
and wild celery.

Every evening he watched his mother
pull young tree shoots
and leafy bushes toward her,
bend and trample them
with her powerful feet
to make their nest for the night.

She arranged smaller leaves
and bushes about her,
and when she settled down
her great weight pressed the springy branches
into a mattress beneath her.

Soon he could make his own nest—
sometimes in a tree,
bending the leafy branches under him—
sometimes on the ground.
But he always left his little nest
to crawl in
beside his big warm mother
and sleep nestled under her arm
or against her round, rumbling belly.

He grew.
Sometimes during the day
he rode on his mother
while the group roamed
through the wet, dense forest
or fragrant meadows,
feeding.

But other times
he walked by himself on the ground,
pulling up his own food,
staying near his mother.
He looked for the prickly thistle
and ate it—
flowers, leaves, prickles
and all. He looked for
nettles and blackberries
and their leaves,
sweet herbs, bedstraw,
and the tender insides of wild celery.
He tried everything.
What he didn't like he spat out.

He grew.
He watched the bigger young ones
wrestle.
When he was a year old
he began to play with them,
to wrestle and roll and
follow the leader.

He was no longer the smallest
in the group.
Now there were new ones,
littler ones,
watching him.
He liked to climb and swing from vines,
to somersault,
to slap his chest
and kick his legs,
to walk across his mother's belly.

Day followed day.
Mist in the morning.
Sometimes rain
sliding off his back as he huddled
with the others.
Sometimes sun
warming their dozing bodies,
gleaming in their blue-black hair.

They kept moving always.
They followed the wild celery
and berry bush, followed
the silvery back of their huge leader
with his great arms
and stiff, crested crown.

The young one grew and grew.
By the time he was three
he was sleeping in his own nest
most of the time.
There were moments
during the browsing
drowsy days
when he felt a tickling excitement.
Then he would toss up leaves and branches
into the air
with quick and furious energy
like the older males.
He began to watch the silver-backed leader
more closely.

One afternoon
when the drops of a brief rain
were still on the leaves,
he noticed a sound,
a soft repeated hoot.
He had heard it before
but it had always been an unimportant noise
like vague and distant thunder.
Now he listened with a new curiosity.
The hoots grew louder and more rapid,
filling him with excitement.

He stopped chewing. He dropped a leafy stalk
he had pulled up
and followed the sound. The swift hoot-hoot
seemed strange to him
in his fascination
yet, at the same time, it was familiar
like the other sounds of the forest.
It came from the clearing where the group rested.
The females and youngsters had pulled into a cluster
at one end. The grown males
paced at the edge near the trees.

In the center of the clearing
sat the great silver-backed one,
his head thrown back,
his lips shaped around the beat
of the sound.
The young one did not join the others
but climbed for a better view
into an overhanging tree.
The air trembled with the silverback's swift hooting.
The great leader reached out
with a light swing
and plucked a leaf from a nearby bush.
He placed it like a flower
between his long, flat lips
and continued to hoot.

The hoots grew louder and faster,
faster and faster still.
Suddenly the huge leader
thrust himself to his short legs.
He tore up great clumps of bush and vine,
tossed them with a furious heave
high into the air,
and began to thump his massive chest
like a frenzied drummer.
The drumming boomed and leapt
into the leafy jungle,
across the high meadows
and jutting cliffs of the rain forest—
an increasing chorus of beats.
The hoots melted
into a blurred growl.

In the meadow
a black buffalo raised his head,
listening.
Birds flew up protesting.
As far as a mile away
a little red forest duiker
bounded nervously into the brush;
a leopard paused in his stalking,
nostrils to the wind.

The young one watched,
the half-chewed food forgotten in his mouth.

Suddenly
the great silverback dropped to all fours
and ran furiously sideways
thrashing his arms and ripping at the ground.
A youngster
who had strayed into the leader's path
was knocked off its feet.
A wild swing of his great arms,
a violent thump on the ground,
and it was over.
Quiet.
The sun shone undisturbed
through the heavy trees.

The bowled-over infant stood up,
shook its head,
and looked around for its mother.
The young one
sat in the tree for a long time afterward,
slowly chewing,
his excitement melting
into the drowsy afternoon.

He was to witness the great silverback's display
with increasing fascination
many times after that.
When the group had been disturbed
by the odor of men
or other groups like themselves
or some excitement he was too young
to recognize,
he came to expect
the leader's violent and compelling ritual.
He began to imitate the lordly crouch,
the great roar.
He even tried the whole kingly ritual himself,
learning to thump the hollow song
from his own expanding chest.
Sometimes
after the mists
had risen and left the forest,
he felt great happiness
in his body.
Then he, too, would thump his chest and toss
great clumps of leaves
high and joyfully into the air.

Day followed misty day
with rains and occasional sunshine.
His hair grew long, blue-black,
and glossy.
He could swing his long arms
and lift himself at a run
into the trees.

He often slept in the trees now,
his nest roughly woven of bent-in branches,
that rested in the crotch of the tree.
His brow had grown jutting
and fierce,
but his eyes were still soft
and brown
like his mother's,
like all their eyes.

When he was eight years old
he was almost full grown.
He was big for his age
and very handsome.
The young females
slapped at him playfully.
Young males avoided him.
On his crown
grew the beginnings
of a stiff, tufted crest
like that of the silver-backed leader.
His body had taken on the heavy muscles
of the young male.
The great silverback began to notice him
with cautious interest,
sensing in the younger
the stirrings of a future lord.

He weighed close to 300 pounds.
He was strong and glossy
and magnificent.

When the hunters came
into the eastern Congo
they were looking for magnificent animals.
They wanted healthy specimens,
young ones.
They wanted the best.
They came from another continent
across the seas.
They wore many clothes
and carried loud weapons.
They hired local trackers,
men from the villages,
to help them catch the wild animals
of Africa
for the people of another continent
to look at, and marvel.

They caught the leopard
and the lion in the bush of the lowlands.
They took the giraffe
from the high grass range,
the hippopotamus from the river bed
and the elephant who had come there to drink at dusk.
And they came into the rain forests
of the highlands,
looking for the mountain gorilla.

It had been an uneasy day,
a close, heavy day
that waited for rain.
The great silverback had led his group
deep among the trees for the night.
They built their nests
with slow, heavy movements
and dropped to sleep.
The young one felt lonely
and disturbed that evening.
He built his nest on the ground
to be closer to the others.

He was awakened abruptly,
jolted from deep in his sleep
by the blood-tingling scream
of the great silverback.
At the same time
he felt the faint slap
of something dense,
yet light,
fall down about him.
Rain?
A web of frozen air?
A net!

The hunters trapped the young one
with a net
among the trees of his own misty forest.
The warning screams of the others
as they escaped
came too late.
With terrifying strangeness
the net closed around him.
He tried to rise but the net tightened,
toppling him from his feet.
He tore at it; he ripped.
He couldn't find his balance.
The more he tore and thrashed,
the more his balance seemed to fail him.
He pulled his own hair in his frenzy.
He heard the great silverback roar and
beat his chest.
But finally
the huge leader dove into the trees,
followed by men making noise
with sticks and guns.

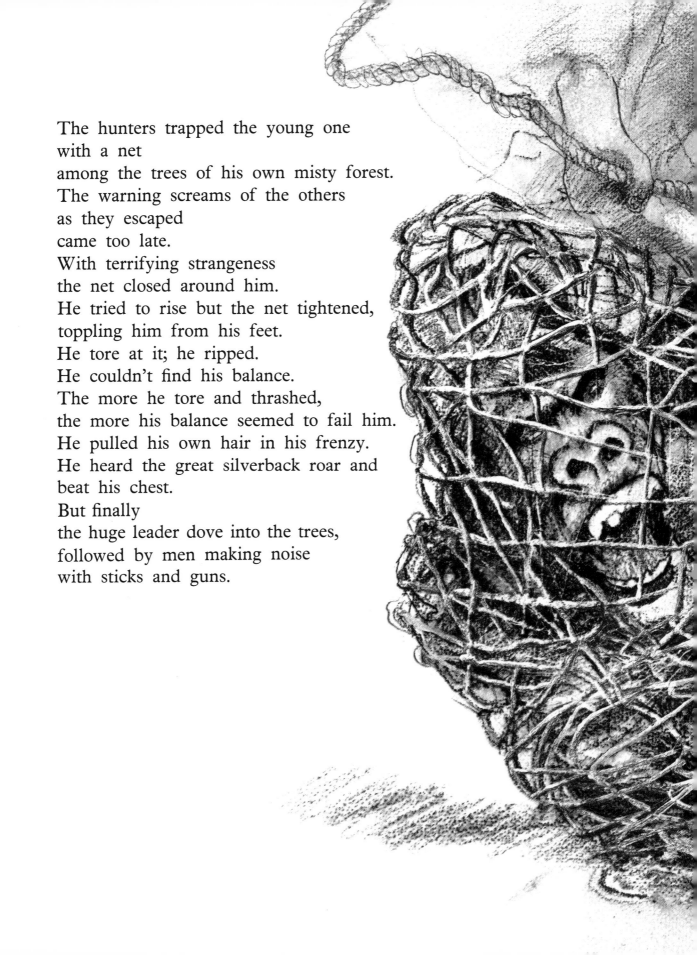

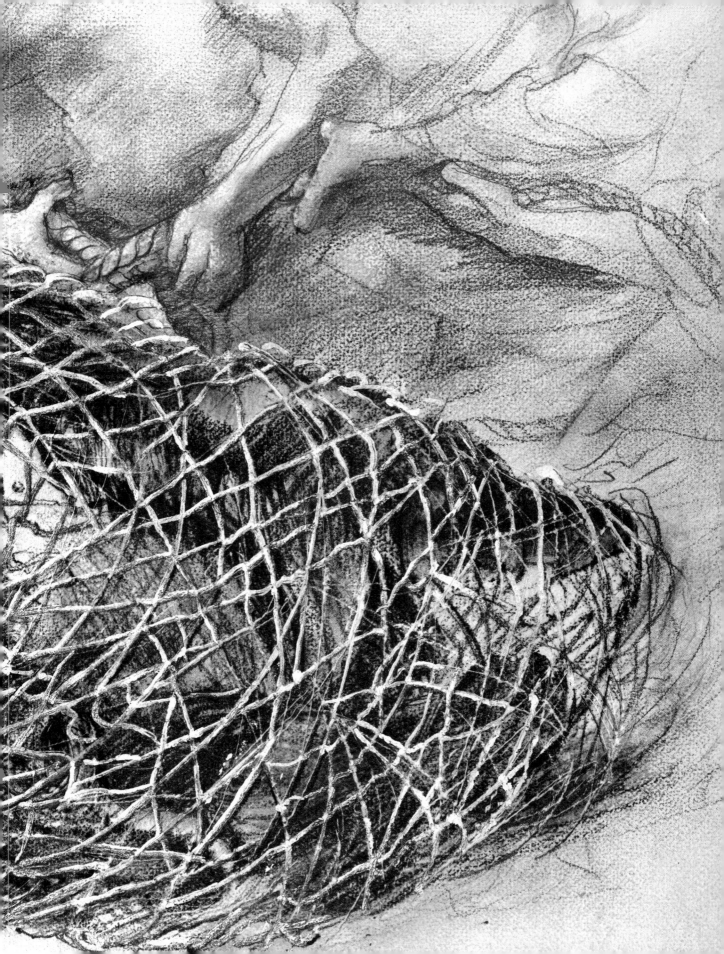

He felt himself lifted,
swaying dizzily. His stomach heaved—
his weight no longer belonged to him.
He struggled blindly in the net.
Then his body touched the floor of a truck.
He was in a cage. Bits of his broken nest
still clung to his hair.
He pounded his big chest
in fury and fear; he grasped
the bars of the cage
and shook them in his powerful hands.
The enemy net was still caught across his shoulders.
"He's a beauty," said one hunter to the other.
And they drove him away
while he raged with the tangled net
in the back of their truck.
From somewhere
deep in the forest
the silverback screamed his warning
over and over.

After a day of sickening travel in the truck,
he was loaded aboard a transport jet
and taken across the ocean
to another continent.
The motion of the plane
made him listless and ill.
He lay on his back
with his legs sprawled
and his soft eyes fixed on the ceiling.
He did not move
except to roll his eyes
toward the man who brought his food.
He did not eat.

All around him was the close smell
of other animals.
Sometimes the tight, helpless growl
of the panther in the next cage
made his sprawled legs twitch.
But he did not move from his back.
When the jet landed,
the big ape's cage
was lowered from the hold
into another truck.
The unfamiliar smells and sounds
of this strange place
made him roll up to his feet.
He clutched the bars of his cage
and peered from under his fierce brow
at the new shapes of things,
at the pale, choppy faces of people.
He was bewildered and sore in his heart.

They took him
to a large zoo.
He was put into an indoor cage
with an outdoor yard
surrounded by high walls and a moat.
There was a tall tree in the yard.
The moat was full of water.
They put a sign
in front of his walled yard.
It said, "Gorilla gorilla beringei,"
and underneath it said,
"Habitat: East Africa."

Gorilla gorilla
did not go outside
into his walled yard.
He lay on his back
in his cage
on the cement floor
with his legs sprawled,
his soft eyes fixed on the ceiling.
He did not eat.

Next to his cage
was a shaggy red orang-utan
who liked apples.
On the other side
were three baboons
who quarreled among themselves
and showed off
for the people
who looked into their cage.

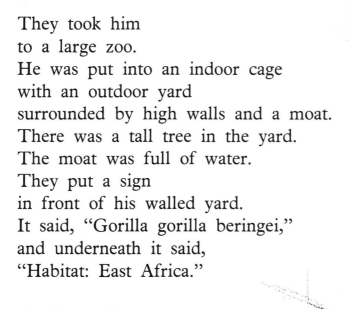

Gorilla gorilla lay on his back
in the indoor cage.
He did not eat.
He stared at the ceiling.

One day
the long, shaggy arm
of the orang-utan
reached through the bars
for Gorilla gorilla's uneaten apples.
Gorilla gorilla turned his fierce brow
toward the orang-utan.
His eyes were angry.
Immediately he rolled to his feet
and slapped the shaggy red arm away.
Orang-utan leapt back with a scream.
Then Gorilla gorilla ate.
He devoured his food.
Later he sat in a corner of his cage
glaring at Orang-utan.

After that he always ate his food.
And sometimes
he went outside into his walled yard
to lie on his back
by the single tree
with his legs sprawled,
staring at the sky.
His hair
began to grow glossy again.

In the afternoons
when school children came to the zoo,
he would lift himself partway
through his door
and leave only his back end
for them to see.
This was not very interesting
to the children.
They always moved on
to the baboons,
who made them laugh with their tricks.
Or they watched Orang-utan,
who climbed about
showing off his shaggy red hair.
No one found Gorilla gorilla
magnificent.

On Sunday afternoons
the zoo was always full of people
peering into the yards and cages.
The panther paced,
restless and frustrated.

The baboons did their tricks
so they could watch the people laugh and clap.
Orang-utan
displayed his amazing shaggy grace.
Sunday was a lively day.
The people watched the animals.
The animals watched the people.
There was clapping and laughing
and the chattering of many voices.

Only Gorilla gorilla
refused to see the people.
He leaned halfway through his door.
All anyone could see of him
was his broad backside.

One day
Orang-utan next door
was moved to another cage.
It took the keepers
all morning to get him out of his old cage.
They finally tempted him out with apples.
For several days
the cage next to Gorilla gorilla
was empty.
He had just begun to miss
his shaggy red neighbor
when the keepers brought in
someone new.

The new one
was another gorilla,
a young female.

Gorilla gorilla watched them
bring her in.
She was sick and listless.
Once inside her cage
she lay on her back
with her eyes on the ceiling.

Gorilla gorilla lay on his back, too,
but occasionally
he stole glances at her
from under his great brow.
Eventually
he stood and paced his cell a while.
He stopped near where she lay in her cage.
He sat down.
She did not move
or look at him,
but he liked the smell from her cage.
It was a familiar smell.
It awakened dim feelings in him.

Fresh rain,
new wet leaves, and damp old wood,
dead trees fragrant with rot and rain . . .
and he smelled his mother
and sun on dozing bodies.
He sat there
with the feel of the rain forest
moving in him.
Old ways stirred his blood . . .
the spongy spring of soft ground
beneath his feet, mossy trees,
and the stretch of his arms
as he lifted himself swinging.

He sat there
immobilized with pleasure,
the warm presence of the long ago group
about him.
In tantalizing snatches
dimly he seemed to hear
the old safe sound
of the great silver-backed leader
snoring in the night.
Inside his chest
an aching swelled.
He rolled restlessly to his feet
and lumbered outside.

It was nighttime in his yard.
He squatted in the darkness,
his soft eyes staring at nothing.
He smelled the great cats
in their close cages.
He heard them twitch
and cough.
He smelled birds on the wind
and elephants swaying on their legs.
The hippopotamus snorted,
and he heard it.
Inside the cage next to his
the young female gorilla
lay on her back,
staring at the ceiling.
Gorilla gorilla's chest ached—
it seemed to him
he was close to home.

The next day was Sunday.
People came from everywhere
to look into the yards and cages.
Parents lifted their children
up high to see.
They threw peanuts
to the elephants.
They watched the panther pace
and the lion lie like a lord.
The baboons made them laugh and clap.
It was a lively day.
The people watched the animals.
The animals watched the people.
There was clapping and laughing
and the chattering of many voices.

As usual
Gorilla gorilla stood half in
and half out
of his doorway.
The young female gorilla lay on her back
inside her cage.
She had eaten nothing.
She did not seem to hear the noise
of people outside.
To Gorilla gorilla
the noise was bright and irritating.
The ache in his chest
swelled.

He looked at the young female.
Her hair
was dull and shedding
and her body
a brooding heap.
She did not admire him.
She was not even curious.
She lay on her back staring
at the ceiling.
Gorilla gorilla stood
halfway through his doorway,
ignored
at both ends.

The noise of people continued
to bother him,
a bright clutter of voices, a scuffling
of feet.
The sounds confused themselves
inside him,
mixed up together
with old sounds he had known.
Sunday sounds of the zoo,
or was it the jungle stirring?
The shrill shout of a child,
or was it a sunbird against the dripping trees?
He heard the caged cat yawn,
the tread of the black buffalo,
the elephant crashing through the brush,
the ice cream vendor, the scolding nurse,
the golden monkey flying through the rain-wet trees,
the rustle that was wild animals
listening
and the jungle growing.

Gorilla gorilla's chest was bursting
with old stirrings
and a new, bewildering ache.
He lifted himself from his doorway
and with a startling heave of his huge bulk,
he turned.
There were gasps from the crowd of people
who had been watching the baboons.
Gorilla gorilla stood leaning
on his knuckles,
staring at them
from under his fierce brow.

The crowd rustled and whispered,
watching the great ape.
Children
pointed their fingers.

Gorilla gorilla sat down slowly;
slowly he tilted his head back.
He parted his lips
and began a low hoot-hoot-hooting,
his gaze fixed in the distance,
like a great silverback
sitting among the vines and bushes
of the forest.
Carefully and deliberately
Gorilla gorilla reached out and plucked a leaf
from beneath his single tree
and placed it delicately between his lips.
The crowd watched,
hushed and waiting.

Then with a startling movement
he hurled himself up and into the tree.
He began to climb,
ripping and tossing branches
as he went.
The crowd gasped
and backed away.
Gorilla gorilla lifted himself
with powerful, easy swings
to the very top fork of his tree.
He stood.
His big hands lifted
and fell,
drumming
against his vast chest.
Again and again.
The deep beat boomed
flat and hollow through the air.

In their cages
the big cats heard
and paused in their pacing.
The elephants heard.
Hippopotamus raised his heavy head.
Inside her cage
the female gorilla
rolled to her feet.
She lifted her head,
her nostrils suddenly alive.

The crowd was silent,
watching the big ape
in amazement.
His huge hands
beat out an ancient sound
against his bursting chest.
Behind him
the sky was pale.
He stood, lifted to his full height
against the light.
"What a magnificent animal!"
said a woman in the crowd.

He stopped drumming
and swung violently to the ground.
He ran furiously sideways,
his huge arms
thrashing out.
He stopped
abruptly
and thumped the ground.
Some people in the crowd
jumped.
It was over.
Quiet.
The sun shone undisturbed
in the pale sky.
They watched him amble to his tree
and sit.
He leaned against the trunk.
He seemed to doze.

Inside her cage
the female gorilla paced.
She was hungry for the first time
since her capture.
She ambled around and around
restless for food,
restless for Gorilla gorilla to return
from his yard
so that she might greet him—
might look into familiar softness
of brown gorilla eyes.

The afternoon grew old.
Children became hungry.
Mothers' and fathers' feet hurt.
Like a sigh
the people began to drift away,
remembering their homes.

Gorilla gorilla
dreamed
against the tree,
a pleasant dream
in which he moved feeding
with the others
among the wild celery and thistles
and in the places of bamboo.

Author's Note

I would like to extend a special thanks to two gentlemen:

George B. Schaller, whose *Year of the Gorilla*
(University of Chicago Press) provided me not only with
facts in my research, but sights, sounds and smells of
the mountain gorilla in his forest.

Jiles B. Williams, my husband, whose excitement over
a magnificent gorilla in the Ueno Park Zoo in Tokyo prompted
the book to begin with.

Carol Fenner Williams

About the Author

Carol Fenner became interested in gorillas while she was living in the Far East, where her husband, Major Jiles B. Williams, USAF, was stationed. They discovered a magnificent gorilla at the Ueno Park Zoo in Tokyo, and she was inspired to study gorilla behavior and write this book. The story was begun in the rocking stateroom of an ocean liner returning to the States. After considerable research, it was finished in Battle Creek, Michigan, where the Williamses now live.

Born in Almond, New York, Miss Fenner migrated to New York City when she was twenty. There she worked at a succession of jobs—as a dancer, actress, teacher, copywriter, and editor. There she also wrote her first two children's books, *Tigers in the Cellar* and *Christmas Tree on the Mountain*. Her third, *Lagalag, the Wanderer*, was written in the Philippines.

At present Miss Fenner is a publicist in Battle Creek, devoting her spare time to tennis, riding the hunt, swimming, and raising "roses, herbs, and things."

About the Artist

Prize-winning artist Symeon Shimin is well known for his illustrations in more than forty children's books, including *Onion John, Dance in the Desert, The Wonderful Story of How You Were Born*, and *Joseph and Koza*.

Mr. Shimin is also well known as a painter. His paintings have been exhibited in various museums, including the Whitney Museum of Art in New York City and the National Gallery in Washington, D.C.

Born in Astrakhan, Russia, in 1902, Shimin came to America in 1912. In order to help support his family, he went to work at the age of fifteen as an apprentice to a commercial artist. Three years later he became a free-lance painter. Although Mr. Shimin studied art at New York City's Cooper Union and at George Luk's studio, he considers himself primarily self-taught. His major schooling was found in museums and galleries here and abroad.

Mr. Shimin maintains a studio in New York City and spends his summers at Amagansett, Long Island, New York.